"Have I Gone Crazy"
Rebecca Davis and ill

Rebecca Davis, through different chapters, reveals her deepest and darkest struggles, but also her greatest and endearing victories of living with the illness of schizophrenia. The book could be described as vignettes for those seeking to know how to successfully survive the symptoms of schizophrenia. Each chapter tells a story of Rebecca's life from her first psychotic break, her hospitalization, isolation, reconciliation with family and friends, and most certainly, her dependence on Jesus to carry her through to victory. The book would be valuable for friends and loved ones of those diagnosed with any of the schizophrenia syndrome disorders, as Rebecca details the physical, mental, and spiritual anguish of experiencing hallucinations, paranoia, rejection, doubt, and suicidal attempts. In fact, the descriptions of these experiences are so real, one may ask themselves, "Am I reading what voices sound like, really?"
As a nursing professor that teaches psychiatric/mental health nursing, I believe Rebecca describes the actual experiences of her symptoms so vividly that my students would gain valuable insight into how hallucinations feel, how paranoia controls one's life and actions, and of how painful the symptoms of schizophrenia truly are through reading "Have I Gone Crazy?" Any healthcare practitioner would find this book to be a credible source for gaining empathy for those with schizophrenia.
It is important to note, that Rebecca gives all the praise and glory to God, the Father, and Jesus, His Son, as the Sources of her victory over the illness and her future hope. She offers valuable verses to

lean on in times of need throughout the hard times of the illness, as well as testimony to answered prayers. The book could also be a great resource for those in the ministry as they council people with schizophrenia or their loved ones.

I also recommend this book for those seeking to read a book about a courageous woman that wants to give her life of pain and suffering and great victory, as a sacrifice to help others and serve the Lord.

Dr. Kathlene Smith – Professor at Tennessee Wesleyan College

Rebecca Davis is a survivor and an overcomer of a disease called mental illness. Through medicine and stubborn faith in Jesus Christ, she has won (and is still winning) major victories over a condition understood by few and feared by many. She holds a Bachelor's Degree in Elementary and Early Childhood education and a Masters in Special Education. She is the founder of His Hands, Inc., a tutoring ministry for needy children.

We overcome thru the blood of the Lamb and the word of our testimony. "Rebecca's words are truly an overcoming message for everyone with a disability, handicap, or impairment – mental or physical. She has won victory thru a veil of tears!"

Linda Gentry – B.A. English

Have I Gone Crazy?

Written by – Rebecca Davis

Cover Illustrated by – Darlene Thurman

Edited by – Anthony Allen, Becky Bevins,

Virginia Bryant, Linda Gentry, & Melissa Marti

His Hands, Inc.
148 Kreis Street
Wartburg, TN 37887
(865) 209-0181
www.hishandstn.org

This book is dedicated to my mother, Wiladean, who insisted that I go to see a Christian counselor. She and my father took care of my daughter, Virginia, and me when I was unable to take care of us. Mama helped me survive the worst struggle in my life.

Have I Gone Crazy?

Part 1 – My Story

Part Two Digging Deeper

Part One

My Story

A Basket Case

The voices in my head were real and kept getting louder. They were the sounds of many aliens all talking at once. Some were speaking at a slow speed in a deep voice, while others raced along at a high pitch. Though I could not understand the words, I understood the harsh ridiculing tone in which these outer space beings spoke. Although I hadn't taken any mind-altering drugs, I was hallucinating.

My sense of touch was also affected. Everything was hard and soft at the same time. My brain became alive with sensations. My cells and organs felt as if I were touching each one. It was as if my internal organs, especially my brain, were extremely soft and hard simultaneously. They were turning to stone and silk; iron and lotion; the hardest hard and the softest soft.

The voices continued to taunt louder, while I was being crushed by the hardness, and smothered by the softness. Fear began to take control. I had to stay calm. Instinctively, I knew that panic would only make matters worse.

Christ had been my source of strength for many years. However, my memory failed when I tried to remember some scripture verses to chase this horrible entity away. Songs were no longer available for recall. I turned on the light and picked up my Bible. My ability to read was gone. Panic began flooding through me. I couldn't let it gain control too. What was I going to do?

I thought that listening to Christian music might help. I got up from my bed and put on a record. I tried to concentrate on the music. It had to drive these sounds and weird sensations away. I settled back into bed. My mother turned the record off. Now what? How could I regain control of my brain? I could still think; but concentration was difficult.

The voices were totally separate from my thoughts. Could they be something real? Was I demon possessed? No, I was a Christian. Christ and a demon could not dwell in the same vessel. I wondered, have I gone crazy? No, I could still think logically. I knew that I was having a hallucination. Will my mind ever come back? That I didn't know. How do I get this to stop?

Streams of hot tears rolled down my cheeks. When I listened to the sounds, they became much louder. They became softer when I tried to concentrate on something else. What could I concentrate on? Thinking was difficult. I whispered the name Jesus over and over, calling upon Him to deliver me. Saying His name brought peace. Over and over I repeated the name, Jesus. I tried only to hear His name, but the voices continued to lash out. But they were somewhat quieted when I said the name, Jesus.

Finally, they were gone. What seemed like an eternity was probably just an hour. I had regained control of my mind. I was exhausted from a day of tension and hours of crying. Sleep came quickly after my fight against being conquered by these hallucinations.

But sleep did not last. After only a few hours, I was awakened by a flashback.

These flashbacks had been happening for months. It was a time of reliving the harsh way that people at school, church, friends, and family

4

members had been treating me. The pictures and sounds of a previously experienced event would enter my mind as though they had a will of their own. I would try to think of some reason for their anger or weird behavior. But the flashbacks left of their own will, just as they had come. A black hole would open in my brain, and a vacuum would suck the images and sounds away. Afterwards, I could only remember generally an event that had happened at school involving a teacher. But I could no longer remember the details. Again, the hot tears would pour down my face. When I was at school, I would run to the bathroom and splash cold water on my face. The cool wetness distracted me, so I was able to go back to teach my class.

At home, flashbacks left me crying for hours. I couldn't face people, so I became a prisoner in my own bedroom. I was locked in my bed for hours with tears streaming from my eyes. I was exhausted by this emotional roller coaster.

Different people would repeat the same words or names to me. Then they would stare in a weird way or snub me. Sometimes my reaction elicited anger, and sometimes it evoked pity. These couplets were totally wrong ways of responding to me, so both reactions caused me severe pain. My brain would hide these thoughts, until the flashbacks would bring two or three events back in a row. While I tried to think of a reason for them, the vacuum would again pull them away.

True or not, I thought people were watching me. I believed that they had even bugged my phone, room, and person. I felt like an experimental monkey in a glass cage with everyone trying to control my behavior.

A trip to the grocery store became unbearable because my mind told me that people were watching me or following me. I thought they watched everything that I put in my buggy, as though there were right or wrong things to buy. As the paranoia would take over, I felt like leaving my buggy and running out of the store screaming. Instead I managed to leave with what few items I had been able to get and check out. But I'd cry, scream, and beat my hand against the dashboard, as soon as I got into the car. At home, I would put the cold and frozen items away, and then collapse into my bed. I was again trapped in my room by the paranoia, tears, and emotional pain.

Even attending church had become too painful to do. As I would sit in the pew, I could feel everyone watching me. The tears would flow all through the service. Usually I thought the preacher was aiming all of his comments directly at me. Eventually, I stayed in my room except for work and grocery shopping.

Although I could no longer attend church, I grew closer to God than ever before in my life. Because of the pain, loneliness, and with no one who understood, I had no choice but to reach up to my Heavenly Father. And His loving presence surrounded me like being wrapped in the softest blanket of love. I would cry myself asleep in His arms.

When I was not crying, I would open my Bible and read. It would fall open to verses that I needed. When my parents had been harsh, I would read about a mother and father forsaking their children but how God would never forsake us. When I was lonely I would read about Job's friends turning against him. Job became my friend who would say, "I understand." When I was suicidal I would read where Paul said, "We were pressed out of measure in that we despaired of life." And again someone said, "I understand."

Finally the school year ended, after I'd used up all my sick days. I took my final Master's degree course that summer; and at first, things seemed better. People appeared to act normal. They did not watch me or try to control me. I managed to stay in one piece during my classes and became calmer. Only near the end of the quarter did the paranoia come back. I reasoned that the church I'd once gone to had gained control of a few people in my college town also. Although the church had disbanded in the spring, I still attributed all my negative emotions to them.

How had it begun? I was attending a non-denominational church which practiced harshly unscriptural discipline on its members. They believed that you could lose your salvation by deliberately sinning. The preacher felt that it was up to the church to keep each member on the right track. In other words, "They played God!" The preacher convinced everyone that I had lied about a female member out of jealously over a man I'd dated. Everyone at church started snubbing me, preaching at me, and spreading rumors about me. The final straw that broke the camel's back was when my fifth grade daughter, Virginia, came out from helping in the church nursery one day. My daughter said, "I don't see why you are mad at Jane."

"I'm not mad at her," I replied. "It just seems like she keeps getting everyone mad at me."

"She has never done anything to you," Virginia replied harshly. "You lied about her."

"I did not lie!" I pleaded. But Virginia only snubbed me. They had gained control of my own daughter and turned her against me. What could I do?

On the way home, I tried to get Virginia to tell me what was said to her about me. She clammed up. I tried explaining that I hadn't lied, but she would not respond.

"If you don't tell me what they said, I'm going to kill myself," I yelled!

Virginia and I both started crying. From that day on, I was suicidal for years. What they had said to my daughter, and my extreme and cruel reaction completely broke our relationship. This added stress to stress.

The pressure, plus an inherited tendency, led me to a complete break. It was apparent to others that I had schizophrenia. My mind, will, and emotions were all a wreck. I became a total basket case.

When school started back, everyone was still acting strangely toward me. But I was convinced that I was not sick. "If everyone would act normal, then I would be all right. I'm not sick. Everyone else is," I told myself.

I had such a large load of children that they hired a teacher's aide for me. She seemed normal but no other school personnel did. I stayed in my classroom and did not even go to lunch. I would still spend most of the evenings crying, having flashbacks, hallucinating, and suffering from paranoia.

I managed to make it through another school year, but I could not continue. I turned in my resignation that spring. I was going to leave this mess, take my daughter, and start over.

I felt that if we moved away, everything would be all right. After all, I had taken college classes in Cookeville. At first, everyone there seemed normal. I thought I'd be O.K., if I could just be around normal people long enough.

Trying to Start Anew

With my retirement funds, I bought a mobile home in Knoxville, Tennessee. Virginia and I moved in that summer. I believed things would be better since I had always been the strongest one in my family; my brother and sister were the emotional ones, not me.

The family members who suffered from a mental illness had broken mentally after the birth of their children. My daughter was in fifth grade before I had any trouble. I was 32 years old before my hallucinations began.

I had gone through the stress of being a single mother without breaking. I'd always managed to raise my daughter alone until the previous two years. When my parents retired and moved in with us, I thought that we would make it just fine in our new home.

I took a job selling Tupperware until I could begin a tutoring ministry. I had planned the ministry for years, but now we needed money to live on.

The flashbacks, hallucinations, and paranoia didn't end. Although the church had disbanded a few years earlier, I believed that Phil, whom I had dated during the time when everyone got mad at me in the church, was still causing all my trouble. I wrote him a letter asking him to release control over me. That was a big mistake. Everything went from bad to totally horrible.

At this time, I had seven or eight Tupperware parties lined up. They all cancelled in one day. Most of them gave the same excuse. I was so angry that I decided to dress up and go to a

11

neighborhood where no one knew me. I would show Phil! I would book more parties.

I worked all day and booked no parties. I cried all night. I was sure that God hadn't allowed me to book any parties because I had the wrong attitude about fighting Phil. I stayed home and cried for several more days. At Tupperware meetings, I felt I was being treated like I had been treated at church and school. My female boss even made sexual advances toward me, which I rejected. This led to me being fired which relieved more problems than it caused.

I tried several other jobs but nothing worked out. The people would start out really nice; however, after a few weeks, I felt like they said words to hurt me, then they would stare, and wait for a response. They tried to control my behavior through snubs or praises at inappropriate times. I was sure that Phil was in control of their behavior. He had also bugged my trailer and phone. There was no escape. He was going to continue punishing me until I died.

When unexplainable things happened, I would come home and cry. The pain was so excruciating that I wanted to die. I would go to the kitchen and take out a butcher knife. The cold, sharp steel would leave an indentation and slight cut as I pressed the knife as hard as I could against my wrist. "It would be so easy to just pull on the handle and it will all be over," I told myself. Then I would pray, "God help me!" He gently, yet forcefully told me that I belonged to Him, and only He had the right to take my life. Then He would bring Virginia to my mind. It would be selfish and so unfair to her if she came home and found me dead.

I'd throw the knife across the room. After a deafening scream, I'd beat my hand against the counter until it swelled to twice its size. It would be so swollen that I couldn't bend the fingers. Only when the physical pain was intense enough to distract me would the suicidal feelings subside. Again, I would find myself in bed sobbing for hours.

Drained of all emotions, I still managed to take my daughter to her activities, cook her supper, keep our laundry done, and keep the house reasonably clean.

When I couldn't get a job, I would sell our things at a flea market and sell my blood plasma. But even at the blood bank, people began treating me awful.

I finally got a part time job at a day care center. It was not enough money to live on, so I would bring their trash home and go through it. I would get out the salvageable scraps for me and the other scraps for Virginia's little dog, Amber. That way I would save the food that I had bought for Virginia to eat.

One day we had so little food in the house that my daughter cried and said, "We are going to starve to death."

I responded, "No, we will not because our family won't let that happen." But I did not believe what I was saying. When I went to bed, I cried most of the night because I had lied to Virginia. Everyone would let us starve unless I could figure out what they wanted and do it. But since I couldn't read minds, I could never figure it out. There was no use telling them that we were hungry. They knew. After all, the trailer was bugged, I reasoned.

I also got very sick physically. Since we had no money to go to the doctor, I continually got worse. My sister had some antibiotics which she offered me. She kept offering but never brought them over. I felt like a dog jumping for a treat, while it was constantly being pulled just out of reach. I grew worse. My lungs hurt, like being stabbed with a sharp knife with each breath of cold air. I coughed up green and brown phlegm. I was totally drained of energy. I knew that I was going to die and that no one would offer help.

One day my sister did bring the medicine. I did not know why. I had not changed my behavior. Why was she suddenly allowed to help me? Nothing made sense, but I took the pills. I improved, but I did not get well for three years. I was left with chronic bronchitis and asthma. It took my breath away every time that I went up steps, tried to sing, or tried to do any work.

We struggled to survive in Knoxville for two years. When Virginia was in eighth grade, she said, "Mama I can't take any more of this. At the Christmas break I'm moving back in with Grandmama and Granddaddy." I agreed that it would be best and helped her pack.

I stayed in Knoxville until the day care replaced me in March. Then I sold the mobile home and moved back in with my parents, also.

Virginia now drew Social Security payments from her deceased father. My parents did not require us to help with the bills so that I could live off the trailer payments. The lady I had sold the mobile home to made $120 payments to me for two years.

14

Getting help

When we moved back in with my parents in Sunbright, Tennessee, I didn't have any bills except gas for the car and doctor bills. I got food stamps from the Department of Human Services so my parents wouldn't have too many extra expenses.

Staying physically alive was easier, but the emotional upheaval was worse. My parents and everyone in the house became the alien monsters who attacked me every day. I felt like they were saying and doing things to deliberately hurt me. Again, I became confined to my own room.

I pretended to be in a concentration camp. The guards were harsh and I was emotionally beaten each day. Wars eventually end so I clung to the hope that one day I would again be free and would again see my family and friends as they once were.

But some days I couldn't hope. The daydream became a nightmare. Green, slimy, outer space creatures had landed on earth and had killed all my family and friends. Then they had taken over the dead bodies of my loved ones, and tormented me. Everyone was gone and would never return. I grieved over their deaths as though they had really died. In my mind and to my emotions, everyone I'd ever known was really dead.

I still had hallucinations and each time it was exactly the same. One night after I'd gone to bed, the voices and the feelings of softness and hardness again came to torment me. By now, I knew that it would last about one hour then be gone. But this time, it was different. After about ten minutes of listening to the outer space creatures, the phone rang. It startled me. I jumped while Mama answered the phone after only one ring. The ringing continued to echo through every cell in my brain. In a few minutes, the ringing stopped and the hallucinations were gone also.

Some days, I would get up in a daze. It was like being awakened out of a deep sleep. Half asleep, I'd have no emotions and I couldn't concentrate on what others said to me. Sometimes Mama would say, "Do you want something to eat?" I'd hear the words, but could not comprehend what she was saying. My mind would repeat, "Do you want something to eat?" over and over until finally I would reply "yes" in an emotionless tone. This fog would last for hours. I couldn't laugh – even at very funny jokes; but on the other hand, I couldn't cry either. The numbness was a blessing, although it made people react stranger than usual. I didn't care. Nothing mattered. I was only awake enough to move – not to feel.

I was still suicidal, but could no longer put the knife to my wrist because people were around. Instead, I would get in my car and drive to Frozen Head Park and hike up one of their trails. I'd plan where I would go off the trail and kill myself with an overdose of something. This made me feel better. It was a way out. I was in control of something. Planning my death actually kept me from doing myself in.

Mama came home from work one day and announced, "I've made you an appointment on Wednesday with a Christian counselor in Knoxville. Here are the directions telling you how to get there. You have to go."

I was horrified. Mama thought I was crazy, but I felt that she really knew that it wasn't me. She knew that everyone else was just persecuting me. I cried, but the appointment was made. I felt as though I had no choice. I had to go, even though I didn't want to. My family was protecting Phil, by saying that I was the one with the problem. On Wednesday, at 11:00, I went to see Josh, the counselor.

I was angry. Josh made a joke about having shrunken heads in his drawer. I didn't laugh. He talked to me. He told me about himself and asked questions. He listened and acted normal most of the time. When he did act strange, he let me tell him about it and apologized. No one else talked to me. They all talked at me to see my reaction instead of to me. It was nice having someone normal around. I felt like I had a friend, even if Mama did pay Josh to talk to me.

Finally, I told Josh about the sounds I kept hearing. He called them voices. Josh said, "You need to make an appointment with a psychiatrist in Oak Ridge. You need medication. It will help."

"But it's not me," I argued. "If everyone will just leave me alone I'll be fine," I cried and begged him to not send me to a psychiatrist.

"If I were in a concentration camp being beaten each day, would you say that medicine would help?" I questioned.

"Yes, it would," Josh said. "I know what the church did to you was real, and I know the pain you feel is real but medication will still help."

Again I felt that I had no choice. I stopped in Oak Ridge at a pay phone. I called Ridgeview and got an appointment.

A few days later, I was sitting in the lobby of Ridgeview. "Rebecca Davis," the woman called. I went with her to a tiny room. Once again I told about the sounds and weird sensations. She called them voices and asked what they said.

"I don't understand them," I said. I was astonished by her appearing to be shocked by my disclosure. "Didn't she get told things like this a lot," I thought.

"Wait here," the lady said and returned a few minutes later with a man. "Tell him what you told me," the lady said.

After I repeated this to him, he said, "Make her an appointment with Dr. Smith." He had no reaction to what I'd told him. It seemed common place for him.

"Come with me," the lady commanded. "Here is your appointment." She handed me the card. I wasn't consulted to find out if that day and time were all right or not. It was just, "here."

The appointment was for three or four weeks later. "If I were really sick, why didn't they get me in earlier? Oh well, I'd go. I had no choice or everyone would treat me horrible," I told myself.

The days passed by, and I went to keep my appointment with the psychiatrist. Dr. Smith listened and then said, "You have schizophrenia. If you don't take your medication regularly, you could have a complete break and end up in an institution for the rest of your life. You will always have to take this medication."

"You don't have to be so harsh," I said. "Patients need compassion."

"You don't need compassion," he replied. "You need the truth."

I stomped out of his office with my prescription for Thorazine. "I'll prove that I don't have schizophrenia," I told myself. "I'll take this medicine and it won't work."

After I got home, I took one pill and settled down in a hot tub of water. I'd cried most of the day and was still crying. After the pill had time to work, I calmed down and stopped crying. For the first time in four years, I was somewhat calm. It felt good. That night I didn't have any hallucinations or flashbacks. It was wonderful.

"But this is awful," I reasoned. "If the pill worked, then I must have schizophrenia." I spent the entire next day looking up articles about mental illness in the encyclopedia. It was true. I did have schizophrenia. But the paranoia wasn't all my imagination. I couldn't separate what had been real from what I'd imagined.

I ordered some free pamphlets from the government on schizophrenia and other mental illnesses. When I got the booklets I read them all. Schizophrenia was just a chemical imbalance; the same as diabetes is. That's why the medication helped to a degree. I was still extremely sick.

The one milligram of Thorazine helped me to stay calmer, helped the hallucinations, stopped the flashbacks, and stopped me from going through my day in a daze. However, I was still suicidal. I still screamed and threw things, was still paranoid, and still cried much of each day.

A few days after starting the medication, I was sitting in the living room watching T.V. All of a sudden, I was lying flat out and spinning around in the darkness of outer space. I could see my arms and legs stretched out. I could feel the spinning

19

motion and I felt myself going further and further into an abyss.

"I'm not really floating in space," I told myself. "I can feel the chair I'm sitting in if I concentrate on it." After just a few minutes, this new hallucination ended. This one was totally different from the others.

I called Ridgeview. Hours later a nurse called me back. I whispered what had happened. She increased my medication to two milligrams.

The medication helped, but I hated the side effects. My mouth was very dry. I had to keep something to drink with me all the time. My eyes were extremely sensitive to light, and my muscles cramped when I over extended them.

Ridgeview gave me Cogentin to control the muscle cramps. It did little to help and had side effects of its own.

A few weeks after starting the Thorazine, I went to Chattanooga to visit a friend. She treated me as if she were one of the aliens sent to torment me. I responded as normally as I could. I didn't cry until I left. She kept saying words that others had said and then stared at me. I stayed friendly and visited all day. That night on my way home, I cried for an hour while driving from Chattanooga to Harriman. I stopped at Kroger in Harriman and went in to get something to drink. When I got back to the car, I took my medicine and headed toward Sunbright.

I remember stopping at the first traffic light in Harriman. Then I entered a daydream. It became palpable and the tangible was gone.

When I came to myself, I was still driving but had taken the wrong fork and was headed toward Oak Ridge. "Boy, I've got to pay attention,"

I told myself as I turned to go toward Sunbright. I again sank into my daydream and didn't remember anything for about five more minutes.

After I got home, I stayed up to watch the 11:00 news. I wanted to see if anyone had been hit or killed on the road I had driven. I was terrified because I couldn't remember anything while driving. I don't see how I stayed on the road. No deaths were reported, so I went on to bed and prayed that I'd not killed anyone or anything.

The next morning I called Ridgeview. The nurse finally called back. "You lost touch with reality," she said and increased my Thorazine to three milligrams.

That was the end of losing touch with reality. No more hallucinations, no more flashbacks, and no more going through the day in a fog, which I learned later is called being catatonic.

Josh said I needed to apply for social security disability. He spent the whole hour convincing me. When I got to Oak Ridge, I stopped at a service station to get directions to the social security office.

The applications were hard to fill out, but it gave me something to do while I was restricted to my room. After several months, I was approved.

I got a large sum for back pay. Mama suggested that I buy a new car. Virginia was old enough to drive now and we really needed two cars. Virginia and I went shopping and bought the car. She drove it to school and I drove it when I had a doctor's appointment or had to go talk to my counselor, Josh.

Josh argued with me. "People aren't really being mean to you. You are just being paranoid," he would say. I'd always cry because I thought he was accusing me of being the bad one. However, I kept going to him once a month.

Becoming Productive

Now that I had an income, I could help my parents with the bills. This made me feel more responsible. It also allowed me to take a writing correspondence course. The course was fun and gave me something to do while I was confined to my room.

When I would get a response back from my instructor, it caused tears and pain because of being paranoid about his negative comments. Nevertheless, I would make myself read it again and realized that most of his comments were positive. "He was just trying to help me," I reassured myself. Then, I'd get busy rewriting a story and doing my next assignment in the writing course.

Even when I wasn't writing for class, I was writing educational, Christian, or children's stories. Staying busy helped me to not cry as much. The course lasted a year or more, so I wrote lots of manuscripts.

After submitting multiple stories to manifold publishers, I began getting a form letter rejecting my work. This didn't bother me though, because it was sent to everyone. I also got a few personal letters commending my work and encouraging me to keep trying to find the right publisher but I didn't sell anything. After a couple of years of continually submitting multiple works, I quit trying for a while. The expense grew too great and I didn't like wasting my time or the publisher's time.

I also began helping around the house. My mother and Virginia were gone during the day, and my father sat up late at night and slept most of the day. I had time to myself. When I wasn't writing, I would wash clothes, do the dishes, or clean up around the house.

Virginia's little dog, Amber, seemed to understand what I was going through better than any human. Amber gave me a lot of comfort. When Virginia got up to get ready for school, Amber would leave her bed and jump up into mine. She would curl up next to my feet. She always seemed to care especially when I was having a bad day. Instead of just lying beside me or at my feet, she would lay her head on my lap or leg and look as if she were going to cry, too. Her behavior told me that she wanted to comfort me. Being a dog, she was kept from being influenced negatively by anyone.

When I watched T.V., Amber would sit in the chair next to me. I also spent time bathing, grooming, feeding, and petting her. Our loving care for each other was a big step toward "normality" for me.

One Christmas, my sister and her husband bought some outdoor paint for my parents' house as a present to them. When spring came, I decided that I would scrape and paint the house. Each pretty day I went out and scraped for about fifteen minutes. Then I came in to rest my cramping arms and drink something for another fifteen minutes. These fifteen minute cycles continued throughout every pleasant day. When I got a large enough area scraped, I would paint it. I worked like this all through the spring, summer, and into the fall.

At the end of each day, I was so proud of what I'd done. My family also began praising my efforts. Occasionally, my mother and daughter would help when they got home in the evenings. We had normal conversations while working. As we worked with our home improvements, they treated me normally. Sometimes this caused stress, too. Having a good time was more than I was used to. I'd been rejected by everyone for more than five years and kindness seemed foreign. Their new behavior would often make me cry, just as well as the anger had. Gradually, I got used to being treated better and cried less.

Finally, one weekend, my sister and her husband, my brother, mother, and daughter all helped and we finished painting the house. That was the first time we'd had a large gathering in which I didn't end up chained to my bed in tears. All holidays, birthdays, and other family gatherings had made me an emotional hostage. The terror of large gatherings always left me crying all night. But this time was different. It was great and we could see the results in a freshly painted house.

It was enjoyable to come out of my bedroom more now. Conversations with my family were more like the pre-break era. Things kept getting better and I had stayed busy. Feeling useful again helped the "daymares" seem like they had only been a bad dream after all.

In the fall, I received a phone call. "This is Bob Jones and I'm with the Right to Life Organization. I just spoke with your friend Sue Harris. She asked me to call you. She is willing to start a Right to Life group in Morgan County, if you will help her," the man said. He promised to help, too.

I said, "I'm not sure I will be able to help."

Bob told me about all the babies that were losing their lives through abortion. He gave me the state and county statistics. It broke my heart for the babies and their suffering mothers. Bob was a good recruiter. I said, "I'll try, but I'm not sure I can help."

I called Sue. She said, "I will help you, but I don't have much time. You will have to do most of the work."

"I don't think I can." I protested. However, a few days later I called Sue back to see what she was willing to do. We both agreed to try.

She got us access to a building in Sunbright, and put an announcement in the newspaper. I called all the country churches to see if the pastors would announce the meeting. All the preachers were really nice, but I had to go slowly. I would call a few and then rest to settle my nerves. After about half an hour, I'd call a few more.

I called Bob back to let him know what we'd done. He agreed to come up and conduct the first meeting. It went well but the crowd was small. Bob showed a film and then asked for nominations for the officers. Everyone wanted me to be the president. If I was not president, we would have no Morgan County Right to Life. I felt it was important, so I agreed to try. Bob and Sue agreed to help. However, I doubted my ability to do the job.

The second meeting was held in Wartburg. We had a bigger crowd. I suggested that someone else be president. No one was willing to take on this job, but all were willing to help in other ways. We had a meeting each month and had several projects. I continued reaching out to people and continued to get better. People were treating me like I was normal, and I responded more normally. I still got paranoid some of the time and cried a lot. But now, I could postpone my tears until after a meeting, event, or activity.

After a couple of years, the Right to Life group decided we should start a crisis pregnancy center in our county. I was elected to the committee to visit other centers in order to learn how to start one. We visited two centers and saw a lawyer. The committee decided that the county needed a family crisis center rather than a crisis pregnancy center.

The county was so poor that we decided to check into the possibility of having a food bank, free pregnancy tests, free baby clothes and supplies, a 24-hour crisis hotline, and a complete referral program for other services. I'd already compiled a large list of organizations with their addresses, phone numbers, and what they had to offer. I'd gotten these from T.V., magazines, radio, and other places over the years. This had been done in hopes of having a list to offer help to the parents of my students when I began the tutoring ministry.

We got everything lined up and placed an article in the paper about the center. All parties interested in helping were invited to attend a meeting. We had a large turnout. I conducted the meeting, and we elected a board. Thankfully, I was vice-chairman instead of chairman. I helped with everything but someone else was in charge. That took a lot of pressure off and allowed me to get better gradually. Everyone knew that I had a mental illness and helped out when I had a bad day. Since I was staying busy and not pushed or under stress, I continued to get better. However, I still wasn't well and I cried almost every night.

One day I saw a Christian video called "The Pineapple Story" Session 1. It told about a missionary and his growth in Christ by learning to die to self and giving up his rights. He began depending on God for all his needs, including friends and his reputation. I responded by deciding to give up my right to have friends, family, and a good reputation. I decided that it didn't matter how I was treated but only how I responded. I acted normal and kind around people even if they were treating me like I was the enemy. I thanked God for everything – the bad as well as the good. I saw this as an opportunity to witness by a calm life. I began crying less and kept being treated better. I learned that if I acted normally, I usually got treated normally. I also quit reacting to my paranoia. I would try to act normal even when I felt like crawling under a rock and hibernating. Even with the paranoia never going away, I could live a somewhat productive and joyful life because I trusted in Jesus, not people.

I trusted that my Lord is always in the boat. He may have been asleep because He knew the boat couldn't go under with Him on board. (Mark 4:37-39) No matter how tempestuous the storm, He would eventually awaken and command the torrents, blazes of fire, and explosive booms to cease. And in an instant, they would obey.

That day didn't happen, but gradually the storms in my soul ceased. I can now rest in complete peace as the storms in my life lessen in severity. I also trust that when my boat is going under that Jesus will hold me in His arms and carry me safely to shore. He has and will always be my wheelchair when I cannot stand.

I'm Not Well Yet

Although I gradually got better, I will always have to take medication. I found this out on four separate occasions.

After taking the Thorazine for several years, my tongue began trembling. The doctor was afraid I was developing Tardive Dyskinesia – a muscle disorder which sometimes develops with long term use of certain antipsychotic drugs. He took me off the medication. "Let's try it without any medicine," my doctor said. "You have been doing a lot better lately."

About two weeks later, I became jumpy. I was startled by a man at the window. When I looked again, it was only a tree branch blowing in the wind.

Later that day, I slammed on my car brakes to avoid hitting a little animal scampering across the road. With a closer look, I found it was just heat waves dancing on the road.

I had not slept well the night before and was extremely tired. It was my day to volunteer a four-hour shift at the Crisis Center. Ann was there, and volunteered to stay. "Go in the back room and lie down on the couch," she said. I did. Just a few minutes after lying down, a large hand reached up and grabbed me. It pulled me down through the couch cushions. I jumped and opened my eyes.

"Boy, that was a weird dream," I told myself. I closed my eyes again and immediately the hand grabbed me and pulled me down into the foam. When I opened my eyes, the gripping sensation, downward movement, and smothery feeling of the sofa cushions enclosing around me instantly ceased. I got up and told Ann. She insisted that I call my doctor immediately. A nurse returned my call very quickly. I went to Ridgeview to pick up my prescription for Haldol. This medication worked, and I had no further problems for two or three years.

However every medication has some side effects. For example, one day I went to see Dr. Little, my dermatologist. He took one look at the rash on my body and said, "It's a chemical rash."

"But I haven't been around any chemicals." I said.

"Do you take any medication?" asked Dr. Little.

"Yes, Haldol and Benadryl," I answered. "But I've taken them for years."

"It's the Haldol," he replied. "You can develop a reaction to it even after years. You'll have to quit taking it."

"But I can't quit, I have hallucinations without it," I protested.

"Call your psychiatrist and see if he can put you on something else," my doctor ordered.

I had already had the rash for a month or more and had seen two different doctors for it. The itching was driving me crazy.

I called Ridgeview. My doctor suggested trying me with no medication for a while.

After about two weeks, I almost stomped my brakes to avoid hitting a little animal scurrying by, only to discover that it was a leaf blowing across the road. When I got home, I immediately called Ridgeview. This time they put me on Stelazine.

The doctor I liked left Ridgeview, and I didn't like any of the other three doctors. I felt trapped by having a doctor that I didn't feel I could communicate with. I went home and called my sister. She lived in Knoxville, and I now lived in Oak Ridge. It wasn't long-distance to call her so I called frequently.

"My doctor left Ridgeview and I don't like any of the other three," I complained.

"Well change doctors," my sister said.

"I can't," I replied.

"Why not?" she inquired.

I didn't have an answer.

"You can call the private psychiatrists in Oak Ridge and see which ones take your insurance. Then you can try them out," my sister continued.

"You're right I will," I responded. I was amazed that the thought had never occurred to me. I didn't have to keep feeling trapped. I could make my own decisions. I had choices. I felt much freer after finding Dr. Rogers.

After about a year of seeing Dr. Rogers, my right hand began trembling. "Let's try you on one of the newer drugs," he said, "They also work better on paranoia. You need help in that area too."

"O.K.," I agreed. One Wednesday night about two weeks later, I came home from church. I'd left my Bible in the car, and I wanted to read. I hurried out to get it.

The air was clean and cool. I loved the sound of the fall leaves crunching beneath my feet. Then I heard the sound of heavier, faster footsteps behind me. I was a little frightened, so I walked faster. The footsteps behind me got faster, also. I stopped and turned to face whoever was behind me. No one was there, and the footsteps had stopped.

I got my Bible from the car and went on to my room. I made a bowl of soup and sat down to eat. All of a sudden, I was moving in slow motion. The spoon went to my mouth in slow motion. I chewed in slow motion, and even swallowed in slow motion. This distortion of time lasted about ten minutes. I immediately called Dr. Rogers and left a message on his machine. The next day he returned my call. Together we decided that I should go back on the Stelazine. It was encouraging to be part of this decision making.

The last episode of hallucinations happened when my drug store chain sold to a different corporation. They also changed the pharmaceutical companies. The new generic Stelazine was a different color and size. That night I couldn't sleep well, nor could I for a month. After taking the new Stelazine that long, I was sitting on my sofa one afternoon. A forest green leaf on my couch became a roach and raced toward me. I jumped and look at the spot where I had seen it. The bug had disappeared. Later a roach crawled across the floor toward the me. When I looked closer, it was gone too.

I called Dr. Rogers and he increased my dosage to 8 milligrams. When it came time to refill the bottle, I changed drug stores. I went back to 6 milligrams with no further problems.

Continuing to Improve

My first goal, before moving to Oak Ridge, was to get back into church. I visited several churches in Morgan County, but never really fit in. Then one day, three of my cousins, who were divorced, said that they wished they had some nice Christian men to date.

"Why don't you go to some singles activities with churches in Oak Ridge?" I suggested.

"We will go if you find out about them and go with us," responded my cousins.

"All right, I'll call the churches tomorrow and let you know," I agreed.

The next morning I called several churches in Oak Ridge and asked about their singles activities. I learned that Calvary Baptist was having a picnic the next weekend at Frozen Head Park in our county.

I called my cousins and we agreed to go. Saturday came. I was a little nervous but I knew that my three cousins would be there. I went and waited for them. They never showed up. All the church members were very nice and I had a good time.

The singles group invited me to a Bible Study they were having on Thursday nights. These studies were at their homes. One of my cousins went with me to several meetings. I kept going and even helped with Calvary's Bible School that summer.

I lived 45 minutes from the church, but after visiting it, I was hooked and had to keep going. It was wonderful to be in an active, growing church again.

Sometimes I was still paranoid. During one activity, I cried for most of the van trip to a play, but gradually I improved and made friends. Friends! Yes, friends were something I never thought I would have again.

When Virginia was 22 years old, she married a young man named Brad. Planning the wedding was fun and brought us closer together. Virginia was a beautiful bride, and Brad has made a very good husband and son-in-law. This was Virginia's dream come true, but it was also mine. Since she had never known her dad, I wanted her to marry a nice Christian man. I got my wish.

After Virginia married and moved out, I started making plans to move, too. I was a lot better now, and my parents needed some time to themselves.

A friend, Clint, lived in a tiny apartment, in Oak Ridge, that was only $180 per month. All the other apartments in his building were bigger and more expensive. Eventually, Clint moved to Knoxville and referred me to live in his old apartment. I measured the spaces and gathered up what stuff I could take. The room had been a janitor's closet converted into an efficiency room for bachelors. The entire 8' x 14' space included a curtain which separated the living room/kitchen from the closet/bathroom. I had a mini refrigerator with a microwave sitting on top of it for the kitchen. Clint left me his sofa to sit and sleep on. A desk for the typewriter and tutoring supplies was across from the sitting area. An end table beside the couch accommodated a lamp. I put up some shelves, above the couch, for dishes. Behind the curtain, there was a shower, sink and commode. Across from them, I moved in a 5-drawer chest of drawers. Two drawers were for clothes, one for canned foods, one for pots and pans, and the thin top drawer was for papers, envelopes, pens, tutoring supplies, etc.

A place of my own was wonderful. Though very small, it was what I needed to move toward seeing my other goals realized. I teased everyone by saying, "Virginia was old enough to move out, so I thought I might be old enough too."

It had been my dream for many years to start a Christian and Educational Ministry. After moving to Oak Ridge, I began to work toward that dream. Helping to start the Crisis Center had given me the knowledge that I needed. My inherited stubbornness supplied the determination I needed. I also believed that God would continue to open doors in the future to see this goal realized.

I asked several Christian friends to be on the board and submitted all the papers I needed to get incorporated and to become tax exempt. His Hands Inc. was born in March, 1995.

My father co-signed for me, and I got a loan to start the business. We published an educational book, Learn Your Times In Five Days. I'd read a book from the library on how to publish your own book and sell a million copies. I did everything the book had said but only sold about half of the 400 books we had printed. I gradually kept working on selling the rest.

I also planned on opening a chain of tutoring ministries which would support one teacher and many volunteers. Parents who couldn't afford to donate would have a businessman sponsor their child and pay for the tutoring.

I called the superintendent's office to get permission to speak to the teachers in each Oak Ridge school. He said, "No, but we will add your name to each school's list of tutors, if you will send us a letter about the ministry."

I mailed the letter and waited for some response. Finally, I called each school to see if they'd received a copy of the letter. They hadn't. I sent a copy to each school or gave information, over the phone, and asked to be placed on their list of tutors.

I put an article about His Hands tutoring ministry and the times table book in the local paper. I called to see if I could speak about the ministry at local churches. The only response I got was, "no." I sent out letters to 100 businesses asking them to sponsor a child but received only negative responses. I spoke at four or five civic organizations. I got no help from them.

After all my work, I got two students which I tutored in my apartment's walking space between the sofa and desk. I sat in a folding chair with a T.V. tray between me and the child, who was on the other side of the tray in another folding chair. This worked well for many months. Then I got a call from a mother needing her daughter and son tutored at the same time.

I had a friend, Lora, whom I'd met after learning to teach a BRIDGES class for people who were recovering from a mental illness. She had been one of my students and was very articulate, well educated, and looking for volunteer opportunities. I asked my pastor if we could use a room at the church for tutoring and he gave me the keys to the old parsonage, which was used for Sunday school classes. Lora wanted the youngest child who turned out to be a boy with ADHD (Attention Deficit Hyperactivity Disorder). She was very patient and good with him, and the young boy and his sister improved rapidly.

We grew rapidly to having nine students. Most of the parents weren't able to donate anything. What little was donated went for supplies and to help pay on the loan, but most of the loan payment came out of my pocket.

Friends from church treated me normally, although they knew about my problem. One time I was talking to my friend, Clint, before he moved. I made a funny remark and he said, "Ah, you're crazy."

"Yes, I know," I responded. "And my psychiatrist can prove it."

We both laughed. It was good to be able to make light of such a serious problem. It was good to be accepted just as I was.

I also dreamed of having speaking engagements where I would share my testimony. I would also do book tours and educational workshops. I have lived some of these dreams. I spoke for the local NAMI Group (National Alliance on Mental Illness). This lead to an opportunity to tell about the illness and read my poetry at the National NAMI Convention, held at the Opryland Hotel, in Nashville, Tennessee. I received a standing ovation after speaking with another lady who played her guitar and sang songs she had written. Imagine me, who would spend the day crying if I were around one or two people, speaking in front of over 600 people.

I have also given my testimony and read my poetry at two separate churches. I would have spoken more, but I couldn't take the stress of being lied to. I had several preachers who said they would call me back and didn't. It really stings when you are disillusioned by pastors acting like the "lost" world. A few weeks later, I called three friends and left messages for them to call me. No one called and at 11:30 P.M., I was a nervous wreck. It took a couple of days for me to recover from the disappointment in believers telling you a lie.

Since publishing my own book didn't work, I tried submitting my work to publishing companies again. I have had some positive feedback from these companies and from friends who have read my material, but no sales. We now publish and print our own works. We do just a few at a time and either sell them or give them to clients who need the books but can't afford to buy them.

I used to be ashamed of my illness because I bought into the lie that it was a weakness in me. Mental illness is no different from any other medical disease. I wouldn't be ashamed of cancer because it would not be my fault. Likewise I have no control over my schizophrenia. It happened to me. I didn't cause it and I can't control it. Medication helps because the illness is a chemical imbalance like any other imbalance in our bodies.

I am not well yet, but I am much, much better. At times I still get paranoid, but it is not as often and only lasts a day or two. I also cry easily, but can usually control it until after I finish what I am doing. When I have a bad day, I cancel everything and take care of myself by going for a walk, calling a friend, or going out to eat. My healing continues because of medication, a stubbornness to keep going, and because my God loves me.

Dreams Come True

The 8 foot by 14 foot apartment was too small. I moved into a larger efficiency so that I could tutor at home. The donated, old computer became a new Dell which was donated by Boeing Aircraft. More Christian and educational books were self-published, and we continued to gain more students.

Finally, I moved into a four room apartment. All the while, my mental illness continued to improve. I no longer have excruciating emotional pain, am not suicidal, am not depressed, and I take my medication regularly. Life is very good. Bad things will always happen on occasion, but Jesus is with me through the storms.

Pressure still takes over at times and causes the chemicals in my body to short circuit my mind. My only symptom when under too much stress is a feeling of an actual sensation in my brain. It is like the sensation people feel when startled, except I feel this in my brain. Now when I am paranoid, I have a sensation in my head like I am actually feeling my brain. Medication, relaxing, and listening to Christian music quickly drives this demon away and again I am able to do ministry work such as tutoring, witnessing, planning and implementing Activity Days, writing, and speaking.

God has really blessed me and the ministry. I had my testimony dramatized on the *Unshackled* radio program, which is heard on the Bible Broadcasting Network. It is too big for me to conceive of, but my testimony was heard worldwide, perhaps by millions.

Joni and Friends played a 5-minute spot about another lady and me who overcame our mental illnesses through volunteering. Thousands if not millions of others also heard this testimony worldwide. Best of all, God opens doors for me to witness one-on-one. He uses me in a personal way. The other person and I can interact. I am always amazed at the wisdom and Scripture verses that my Father gives me when witnessing. My life is more productive now than even before the disability developed.

It was a dream come true when we had 21 kids at our Fall Festival. There were three teen workers and 13 adults who worked along with us. This was our biggest Activity Day for children yet. God has given me a vision of even bigger and better things. Whether ministering and witnessing one-on-one at a doctor's office, the hair dresser, in my apartment, or speaking before hundreds my life is very fulfilling.

I have accomplished large goals like *Unshackled* and have spoken to about 600 people at the NAMI (National Alliance for the Mentally Ill) National convention. But I also accomplish small goals like taking a lady to her doctor's appointment, tutoring one at a time, and talking on the phone to someone who is upset. This gives me a sense of purpose. No matter what the results, I trust God to use it all for His glory.

How did I go from crying all day and being suicidal to seeing my dreams come true? First I decided that I could not control how I was treated or what happened to me. But I could control, with the help of Jesus, how I responded.

Without God, people's treatment of me and my mind's reaction may have locked me in a nightmare with no way out! However, I can choose to love even if I am not loved back. I can forgive even if I am not forgiven. God's peace and joy are mine, even in the middle of a storm. Having a good day is always a choice, but during the quietness of night, the flashbacks take on a life of their own when the day was too stressful.

I quit crying all the time and started being happier. In turn, people started treating me better. Even when treated badly, my peace is restored quickly. Although schizophrenia is a nightmare that I will always be locked in, I can choose to make it a comfortable place. For the most part I enjoy my life, am a contributing part of society, helping to make life better for others, and joyfully serving my Lord.

The second thing I learned was that we should accept life as it is, not as we want it to be or dream of having it as it used to be. But don't just resign yourself to a helpless or hopeless state. Keep striving to better things. Keep working on relationships. The first is with Jesus, then with others, and finally with yourself. If you know you are who God wants you to be, then you can be happy even if people don't like or approve of you. If God is all you have, then God is still enough.

I quit being suicidal. Satan can no longer tempt me to take my own life no matter what or who I lose. Why? Because I gladly lose all to serve Christ. My suffering was not in vain because now I "know Him and the fellowship of His suffering," and I am beginning to know the "Power of His resurrection." (Philippians 3:10)

Third, I came to know deep down that God loves me more than anyone else could ever love me. He loved me enough to send His one and only begotten son, Jesus, to die in my place, to pay for my sins. GOD is in CONTROL! He was in control when He allowed Jesus to die on the cross and He is in control when he allows bad things to happen in our world today. God loves me and He is in control. Everything that I go through has a good purpose, even the really bad things. All I had to do was trust that my Lord knows what He was doing. Yeah, Really! Sounds easy but it took years to trust Jesus when my boat was going under. Finally, I got to the place of believing and using II Corinthians 1:3-9. Verse 4 says, "Who comforteth us in all our tribulation, that we may be able to comfort them which are in any trouble, by the comfort wherewith we ourselves are comforted of God."

God was always with me. He used Job, Paul, Elisha, and others to comfort me as well as a little dog named Amber. He saw me through my situation. At the same time, He answered my prayer to be a vessel which is useful to Him. Talk about answered prayers – *Unshackled, Joni and Friends*, and every day ministry. I see miracles all the time and do and say things that I never thought possible. God indeed is love and everything He allows is for our good. God doesn't cause evil – the devil does. God allows it because he can see a greater good coming from it.

The second best dream to come true is that my relationships with my daughter, son-in-law, and two granddaughters, Allie and Sydney, are growing each day.

The first best dream that has come true is that my relationship with Jesus is much stronger now. It is not contingent on what He does for me but on a simple faith that trusts Him no matter what. Even when locked in the prison of paranoia, my

Lord is with me and makes the dark, damp, dungeon of mental illness light up with purpose.

Since I have been at the bottom of the pit, the good times seem sweeter. Now my mind races with dreams waiting to be fulfilled. I praise Him for those dreams which have already come true and for the ones He is still working on. When God paints a life, He uses all the colors, the dark ones as well as the bright ones. My life is becoming Christ's beautiful masterpiece.

Psychiatric Hospital

Flashbacks, crying for days, and suicidal thoughts came again. I'd thought it was over forever. But, **NO!** The psychiatric hospital would be my new prison for seven days. As bad as I'd been before, I had managed to stay out of the hospital.

The nurse interviewing me abruptly stated, "We have someone else coming in about an hour so just answer the questions as briefly as possible. We'll have plenty of time to get to know you later."

After the interview, I was seated on one side of the desk while the attendant went through all my clothes and things. The paper sack was for what I got to keep, while the contraband was put back in my suitcase to be locked away.

"You'll have to take your tennis shoes off. Here are some footies you can wear while you are here," the attendant demanded as he continued going through everything and itemizing my personal belongings.

"Rebecca!" a familiar voice shouted. I looked while Lucy hobbled her way toward me on her walker. "I have been praying for two days that you would come here!" Lucy eagerly exclaimed.

"Why, God did you have to answer her prayer like this?" a quick prayer went up from within. I'd been crying and suicidal for two days. This was no coincidence. Lucy and I talked, and I encouraged her. Consequently, this encouraged me.

Finally, after a strip search and a rough medical exam, I was shown to my room. "Plop," you could hear the thick fire proof cover and rock-hard mattress core barely give with each turn of my body. I tried to find some elusive comfort.

"What are you in for?" were my roommate's first words.

"You make it sound like prison," I replied.

"Well it is!" she exclaimed. Jessica was easy to talk to. By the time that she left two days later, we had revealed to each other our life stories.

It was nice not having a roommate for a few days, even though I had liked Jessica and enjoyed her company. The occasional solitude made it easier to find time to spend with God. We had lots of groups to attend. We had a significant amount of literature which we were encouraged to read. During the morning group, we had to establish goals which we were required to attempt to achieve. Since physical exercise helps to elevate one's mood, my first goal was always to walk a mile around the hallway. Since I struggled greatly in my emotions due to the loss of both the perceived and actual support of my family and friends, I set goals which were related to grief recovery and to the development of relationship-building skills.

Stacy was sitting in her wheelchair but kept it moving with her feet. She was being really loud and obnoxious the day that I first arrived. She kept yelling, "Can I get out of this wheelchair?"

"Not until the doctor orders it," was the same response she kept getting.

She said loud enough for everyone to hear, "But why do I have to stay in it?"

The reply was always, "Because you fell. Quiet down, there are other people to consider."

"I'm not bothering anyone. Am I bothering you or you?" she'd yell in our faces.

Everyone but me snubbed Stacy. I tried to make friends with her, and I sat and talked with her at times.

During meals she always ate by herself. A few times I tried to eat with her, but she sent me back to the table with the rest of the group. Everyone talked bad about Stacy except me. One day I had something kind to tell the rest of the group about her.

The night before, I'd been in my room crying for over an hour. Stacy was out of her wheelchair, and I saw her quietly standing in my doorway. "Can I help?" she softly asked. We talked a few minutes. Her sympathy was genuine and not a ploy to get attention. She didn't share what I'd said with anyone else. After leaving my room she was quiet for a while. But, then she returned to her usual self.

Stacy handed me a piece of paper and said, "Here is my phone number. Call me when you get out." Several people were going home and exchanged phone numbers. I was the only one who got Stacy's number, and I was grateful for it. We had several good conversations before she moved. But, we lost contact.

During groups, when we talked about what helped, I always told about my relationship with Jesus and how I always found comfort in Him. Jack, who had been there for alcohol and drugs, said, "Rebecca, I want to talk with you while the others go out to smoke. Every morning, I have been encouraged by your smiling face when we come out for vital signs and meds. I've listened a lot while you talk about Jesus. You won't believe this but I was once happily married, had a family and even taught 10 and 11 year old boys in Sunday school.

You are one reason I'm going to an A and D program long term. Now that I'm detoxed, I want to get my life back and teach the 10 and 11 year old boys' Sunday school class again. I think I can help make some boys to not make the same mistakes that I've made. Thank you for your help." I'm sure he reached his goals, because he was seeking help from the only true source of help – God.

Oscar, an older man, sat with me after lunch the next day and told a similar story. He'd been saved as a boy and gone to church regularly until his divorce. His kids, grandkids, their boyfriends, and girlfriends had all moved in with him. Drugs, alcohol, and fighting were their lifestyle. "Rebecca, I'm leaving. The case worker has helped me find an apartment for elderly and disabled people. I'm not going back to that mess. When I came here I wanted to die. Now I want my own place, peace and quiet, and to get back into church. Last night I rededicated my life back to God because of some of the things that you said. My life is going to be different."

"Oscar you will never know how much you have helped me. God bless you," I responded. These encouraging words helped me more than anyone could ever imagine. A day or two later I went home and resumed tutoring.

Lucy had gone home several days before me. We'd made a pact while in the hospital: "We'll remind each other every day to take our medication and be buddies to help one another stay well." Lucy was back off her medication. It would be years later before circumstances and God would get her on her meds to stay. Being evicted, becoming homeless, wandering the streets, not eating, developing a diabetic sore on her leg, and being found by two strangers along the interstate got Lucy in the

48

psychiatric hospital. She was put in a transition house long enough to realize that she needed the medication. She has been stable for years and praises God for all those who have helped her along the way.

God used the prayers of Lucy to get me where He wanted me. My depression, tears, and suicidal thoughts may have been caused by Satan putting too much stress on me, but God allowed it. He allowed it for lots of good. He allowed it for Lucy, Stacy, Jack, Oscar, and me. "For when I am weak, then am I strong." (II Corinthians 12:10) I'm not strong in my strength, but in His.

Praise God, He truly does, "Work all things together for good to them that love the Lord and are the called according to His purpose." (Romans 8:28)

Part Two

Digging

Deeper

Why?

Why did I go to a church that disciplined its members harshly? Why did I date the deacon, who was my boss at work? Why did my whole world crash in? Why did I lose everyone's love and support?

The answer is so that I could grow in Christ to the point that I could be an empty vessel for Him to use. My strength is made perfect in weakness. (II Corinthians 12:9) When I am weak then I am strong. (II Corinthians 12:10). Christ's strength is perfected in me because there is less of me left.

Right before everyone thought I'd lied about a friend at church, I'd prayed a Scripture verse, "That I may know Him and the power of His resurrection and the fellowship of His sufferings, being made conformable unto His death." (Philippians 3:10). In essence, I prayed to suffer as much as Jesus did. Impossible? True. He took all my pain and sins, all Job's, all Hitler's, all Judas' and all yours. All the trillions or more people that have ever lived or will ever live – Jesus took their sins and pain.

My pain was more than I could stand, so my mind, will, and emotions all broke. People say, "God won't put more on anyone than they can stand." They are misquoting a Bible verse. That verse says, "God will not tempt you above what you can stand but will with the temptation also make a way of escape so you can bear it," is my paraphrase of I Corinthians 10:13. That means there is no excuse for sin because we have a way to escape it, which means depending on Jesus (in me) to keep me from sinning. Huge numbers of people have suffered more than they can stand. But Jesus is in the business of making the broken whole again, even with the help of medication. Plenty of martyrs had to face more than they could stand. Am I a martyr? Hardly! I am just a child of God who wants to be His complete vessel, completely empty in His Hands awaiting Him to fill me and pour me out on all He loves, which is everyone.

Before I broke, I was interested in housekeeping, being the best teacher and mother possible, serving God, growing in Him, and doing a tutoring ministry when I retired. But God had different plans. Wham! I was living a normal life one day, and in a matter of weeks I was totally engrossed in my pain and totally reaching to the only one I had left – JESUS!

Would I change over 30 years of mostly living in a nightmare for the closeness I gained to Jesus? No way! Would I choose to do it again? No way! I barely survived once. I'm not sure that I could survive again.

How much was paranoia and how much was real I will never know. I do know the church discipline was real and 75 other families left because of it. I can do nothing about their pain, but what now matters is that I know Jesus more each day and have a great hope for the future. God allowed it all for a purpose, a good purpose.

The hallucinations are gone. The flashbacks and weird feeling in my brain are gone. The paranoia still comes at times but it no longer controls or depresses me. I have learned to not try to do things but to just allow God to do them through me.

The church that broke me also helped me in several ways. The music all pointed to Jesus and growing closer to Him. The people fellowshipped a lot unless they thought you'd sinned. I learned a lot about loving my Christian brothers and sisters through their behavior. They were sincere in their belief that you can lose your salvation. That was what caused them to snub people, which is sin. The Bible plainly says, "My father holds you in the palm of His hands and no one can pull you out." (John 10: 28-29 – my paraphrase). It is God's responsibility to save and to correct us. The church members played God, and therein lay the sin which broke lots of lives, especially those doing the discipline. Our job is to show God's love. "It is the goodness of God that leads men to repentance." (Romans 2:4).

The people at the church were good at allowing members to do new things in service to God and in encouraging them. I asked the pastor, "Can I do a short children's service on our Wednesday family night's service?"

"That would be great, Rebecca," he said. You are especially good with children and your teaching experience could help."

The old building that we met in leaked, but no one seemed to mind. Many people came early to mop up, put out buckets, and move chairs away from leaks. Virginia and I drove 45 minutes to church so we stayed over for night service. We were given a key to the church for a place to stay, but rarely used it. "Rebecca, will you and Virginia come to our house between services? We've got a roast cooking and our kids can play while we visit," someone would always graciously ask.

Everyone at church was given a chance to testify, sing, or speak a word from God and we always clapped for the person speaking up. In fact, I was growing in Christ before the mental break. I sang the songs with all my heart. They too, were sung as prayers. Here are three of my favorites:

Lord, prepare me,
To be your sanctuary.
Pure and Holy,
Tried and true--
With thanksgiving,
I'll be a living,
Sanctuary, for you.

I love you Lord,
And I lift my voice,
To worship you,
Oh my soul rejoice.
Take joy my King,
In what you hear.
Let me be a sweet sweet sound,
In your ear.

I was born to be your dwelling place,
A home for the presence of the Lord.
Let my life now be,
Consecrated Lord to thee,
That I might be what I was born to be.

When singing these songs, I could picture God using me mightily and indwelling me fully, for His glory. My experience at this church plus mental illness was God's way of answering my prayers. Why did He choose to answer them in a way that seemed so awful?

1. To end a church that was hurting people.
2. To cause the pastor to return home and hopefully reconcile with all of his family.
3. To make me totally dependent on Jesus.
4. To give me time to spend with God and in ministry.
5. To take the world out of me, and to put His desires in me.

I thank God for all of my past, even the times that were nightmares and "daymares." I can now reach down in the gutter and pull a homeless man who has a mental illness out by telling him, "I understand and Jesus loves you." I can reach out to a single mom and say, "I have been there too. Let me introduce you to someone who will treat you like a lady and never require anything in return. He loved you so much that He died for you."

I can visit with educated professors because I have a Master's Degree. That degree pales beside my adoption papers told about in Romans 8:14-17. I was adopted by the King of all kings. I am now a royal princess. No, I'm not egotistical. All who accept Jesus' gift of forgiveness from sins are His children. He died to take all our sins upon Himself and to give us all His righteousness. Real salvation always produces a life change. It may take time, but yielding your life to Jesus produces the change because He moves in and helps you transform into a royal prince or princess. He helps you become who you were born to be. That new person is someone that you always wanted to be deep down in your heart. When you repent of your sins, accept His gift, and invite Jesus into your life. You too can become a prince or princess.

Why? Because God can see the future and we can't. In the Old Testament, God needed to teach Joseph to be a leader. He did this by allowing Satan to have him sold into slavery in Egypt. God blessed Joseph to be over the entire household of his master as well as the other slaves.

Next, Joseph went to prison, and God again blessed him by allowing him to be put over the prison and prisoners. God wanted him there as a stepping stone to the palace of Pharaoh. When two of Pharaoh's servants were thrown into prison, they both had dreams while interred and God gave Joseph the interpretation. Both dreams came true – the baker was hanged and the cup bearer was restored to his position. He promised to tell the king about Joseph, but forgot about him.

Once again it was God's timing. When seven years of plenty would be followed by seven years of famine, God sent Joseph to the palace to save everyone in the region, including his own family. When God brought Joseph out of captivity, He made Joseph second in command in Egypt. (Genesis 37:1-36, 39:1-47:27) Read this story! It is historic reality.

Why? Because, God knows best. He knew best in Joseph's life and He knows best in my life. He is opening new doors which will use all I have been through for His glory. When He closes doors to ministry, I get more planning and writing done. When He opens doors to ministry, people can see Jesus in me. I am too weak to do what He has called me to do. Going from not being able to get out of bed or meet my own needs to doing a large ministry is amazing. All I can say is to God be the glory!

Learning Experiences

Before developing a mental illness, God told me to begin a tutoring ministry. After my break, I was too sick to do anything. However I did manage to tutor one girl for a short time.

Each step of the way, God was working. When I didn't have money for food, God provided cans to recycle, coupons from my sister's old newspapers, two double coupon stores close by, and many bags of groceries for only a few dollars. The newspaper also had ads to sell blood plasma which provided money for food and gas.

Once my daughter cried because we were out of milk and tearfully bemoaned, "We are going to starve to death." My efforts to reassure her failed because I also believed we were going to die. God intervened with hope when He reminded me of all the pennies I'd vacuumed up when we first moved in. I grabbed the vacuum and listened as I heard ping, ping, ping, while the nozzle ran across the wallboard and praised God at the rapid fire of pennies shooting into the vacuum from the heater vents I'd taken the grates off of. I cleaned off the pennies and headed to the store. There was enough to buy a pint of milk, with a few pennies left over. Even though Virginia drank to her fill every day, the pint lasted the whole week – God not only multiplies fish and bread but also milk.

I learned to stretch a dollar in many ways: using 15-watt light bulbs; no cable TV; turning the heat down in winter and wearing coats indoors; and turning the air up and dressing light in summer. These experiences led to a workshop called "Stretch

Your Money." There are plenty of financial workshops for the rich or middle class but none for the poor until now. God doesn't waste anything that we go through but uses it for His glory and to help others.

Beginning the Right to Life group gave me experience at talking with pastors about church outreach. I was able to be out in public again.

Starting the Crisis Center taught me the most. I learned the legal paperwork by going with two other ladies to meet with a legal aid attorney. Going to classes about starting crisis pregnancy centers, suicide intervention classes, and other classes helped both then and later in the ministries that God has given me. I taught Parenting classes for DHS for years and also for an Alcohol and Drug rehabilitation program. We had some positive feedback through letters and seeing ladies in public with their children. "We are in church now and I have a good relationship with my daughter now," they would say. Encouragement like this made it all worthwhile and helped me to understand that I have always been in the center of God's will, even when crying for days.

After opening the Crisis Center, we saw many miracles happen. When our food pantry was low, we would pray and the boy scouts would bring a pickup load of food, a church would bring box after box of food that they had collected, and one poor man always brought two cans of food every Monday morning.

Miracles happened on our phone line and when clients came in, too. We had crisis calls which always seemed to come when the best person to deal with it was on duty. God had taught me to trust Him when my daughter and I moved back to

Tennessee from Georgia, and I was getting to see the results of that trust.

One day I had worked a 4-hour shift and was about to put the calls on call forwarding, I dialed the lady on duty and got no answer. That was unusual, so I started to dial again. A voice in my head said, "She is not home, put it on yourself. You will have a call tonight." I tried again to reach her and heard the same voice, so I set the phone on me, then went home. Soon after I arrived home, Scarlet (the lady on duty) called, "I forgot to tell you that I am out of town and won't be able to take calls tonight."

I told her, "No problem," and described what had happened. I knew I was going to get a call, so I stayed dressed and waited up. The call came around 10 or 11 P.M. A teenager lived with her uncle who sexually, emotionally, and physically abused her. He had pistol whipped her on the head and threatened to kill her that night. She wanted me to come get her. I wouldn't go to her home but she told me about a mini-mart she might be able to get to in an hour. I called the YWCA shelter hotline and made arrangements for them to meet us after I got her.

I waited an extra hour after time for her to show up then decided to leave. The same voice I'd heard earlier said, "She is trying to come, stay as long as you need to stay."

From that point on, I prayed and waited peacefully. After about another hour a car drove up and a teenage girl jumped out with a suitcase. "Are you Rebecca?" she hurriedly asked.

"Yes," I replied as she jumped into my car.

61

"Let's get out of here before he changes his mind," she commanded.

We pulled onto I-40 and he followed us. She started screaming.

"Calm down. I'll take the next exit and go to the police station," I encouraged. All I had to do was pull into the police parking lot and he sped off. We waited there a while. I called the YWCA hotline again. They said to come on. They would stop at the police station again if he followed us. They were also sending a male volunteer to help in the car switch.

No one followed us and after midnight we met the car at the Y. A police car was sitting beside it. The switch was made and the teenager was taken to a safe, undisclosed location.

Miracles like this one happened on an almost daily basis, if not more often than once a day. My faith increased, and now I can trust even when the bad happens.

God also taught me much about Him being no respecter of persons. We dealt with alcoholics, others with mental illness, pregnant teens, girls who had abortions, homeless, and dirty people. With each one, God broke down walls in my life.

Bugs always made me tremble. I could love dirty people but had a problem touching them. Just before leaving the crisis center one afternoon in mid-winter, we got a call. A lady's gas furnace had gone out in her mobile home. There was no heat or water, and the temperature was going to be below freezing that night. She could get water from a nearby fire hydrant, but needed an electric heater. A large freestanding electric heater had been donated just that week.

I lived in Oak Ridge now so it wasn't much out of my way to drop off the heater. I drove up a mud and gravel driveway. The yard was pure mud with ooze-soaked 2'x 4' planks laid out to walk on. The lady waited on the porch as I balanced on the slippery planks and carried the heater up to her. Her matted, unwashed hair matched the mud and soot that streaked her face and bare arms. She poured her heart out to me as I searched my purse for a clean tissue to dry her tear-soaked face. My show of sympathy overwhelmed her. She grabbed me with a bear hug and buried her face into my shoulder which sopped up her tears and runny nose. God said, "Hug her back." I prayed for forgiveness and instantly God broke my heart. I embraced her and we hugged and prayed together for about half an hour. She told me of all their misfortune. "Call us anytime," I encouraged. But God saw fit to help them through other means. I left feeling free of judging others because of dirt and mud.

My first friend who committed suicide taught me a lot about people and God. God, not Satan, is in control. Millie usually called late at night and told me, "I'm going to kill myself, right now! I've got all my medication and I'll be dead before you can get here."

"Millie, please talk to me. God loves you and so do I," I'd plead.

After talking about what was bothering her, I'd drive the dark roads half an hour to get her and drive another hour to take her to Saint Mary's Hospital. I would spend an hour of talking with Millie about God's love and her problems. She would grow quiet as she fell asleep, safe in the hospital emergency room. Mobile Crisis would finally come. The hours continued to drift by as we waited for her to be admitted to their psychiatric unit. Getting home only an hour or two before daybreak made me unhook my phone, turn off the alarm and sleep most of the following day away.

The invitation was continual, "Millie will you go to church with me tonight?"

Her "Not Now!" finally turned into "Yes." After much time of hearing about Jesus at church and in our conversations, Millie raised her hand to signify her praying to yield her life to the Lord. Millie's depression was less and she eagerly talked about Christ.

A few months later, Millie called from the Mental Unit at Saint Mary's. "Rebecca, will you bring me a pack of cigarettes tonight?"

"Not this late," was my response.

At first Millie begged, then she angrily screamed, "I'll never call you again," and slammed the phone down.

We did talk a few times after that and I thought she trusted me to help again. But one rainy night, Millie fussed with her mother. She sped off to her grandmother's home. They too argued. Millie's usual behavior would have been to call me, but this time her suicidal thoughts had her drive to an empty parking lot, swallow all her medication with a soda, get out of the car, and lay in the rain as she waited to die.

Early the next morning, the store manager found her lifeless, rain soaked body, lying beside her car. I questioned, "Why didn't I just take her the cigarettes?" But God reassured me that I had done all I could have done. I knew that she had truly given her life to Jesus, and that God took her home even if her final act was disobedience. She left behind many hurting people. Even though she was in Heaven, she would suffer loss because her last act was very selfish and a slap in God's face. No one has the right to take their own life because Jesus purchased God's forgiveness for everyone on the cross.

Years later, my pastor put what I felt into words at a funeral of a young man who suffered from untreated schizophrenia. Although he had killed himself, God through my pastor very wisely said, "Don didn't kill himself, the illness did."

That is so true. If I could do something different in all the lives of friends who have committed suicide to have prevented it from happening, I would. God has shown me that there has never been anything else that I could have done. My main goals have always been to be there for the people who have given up on themselves and on life. Many people have told me that they have lived many more years because God was there through me, when no one else was there for them. Many people also gave their lives to Jesus because of the seeds He planted in their lives through me. Some went on to commit suicide and others are still alive and growing in Christ. I can't control another person's actions any more than I can control the weather. God ultimately is in control even when it seems like the devil is. We just go when God says go and leave the results to Him.

Those who died not receiving Jesus are not my responsibility either. We all have free will. If I could choose Christ for everyone, I would. But, each person must receive Him for himself or herself.

If God, looking through time, had seen a point in that person's life where he would receive His Son, then Satan could not have taken their life at that point. II Peter 3:9 says, "The Lord is … not willing that any should perish, but that all should come to repentance." God gives all men the very last chance to come to Him. Even at the point between life and death some have given their lives to the Lord. We, on this side of eternity, can't always know the deceased person's eternal place, but God gave them every chance, even while unconscious. So, I trust in God's patience, love and mercy, not in what I see or feel.

I heard a young home missionary tell of coming home from high school at the age of 16 to find both her parents at home. They confronted her with the awful reality that they were divorcing and that she had to choose right then who she would live with. Her dad, packed and ready to leave, wanted her to come with him. Her mom begged her to stay. The pressure was too much. She ran out the back door, with tears streaming down her face, only stopping long enough to grab a knife from the kitchen drawer. In a cornfield, while sobbing out of control, she slit her wrist. After passing out, she heard Jesus call to her, "Beth, get up. I have other plans for your life." While still unconscious, she said, "Yes Lord, I'll do whatever you want me to do," and she surrendered her life to Jesus. Beth came to and struggled to the road, where she passed out again. An oncoming driver stopped, scooped her up, and took her to the hospital. Beth was saved because she didn't choose her mom or dad, but Christ.

After all God taught me at the Crisis Center, He finally had me open the tutoring ministry. His Hands, Inc. was instituted. The paperwork came easy, after what I'd learned at the Crisis Center. Trusting God for the needed supplies was just like trusting my father as a child to meet my needs. After seeing so many miracles at the Crisis Center, God still continued to provide. Books, including encyclopedias, were donated by a couple marrying from my church. They were downsizing to combine two families. Later a private school was closing, and many educational supplies were donated, including a reading series through fifth grade. Miracles have continued throughout this endeavor.

The tutoring began in my 8' x 14' apartment with two students. Soon we moved to a room in my church's old parsonage. We tutored several more students as word of mouth caused the ministry to grow.

At the first Activity Day, we only had one student show up. Sarah, a ninth-grade girl, was working on a seventh-grade math level. She was quite a bit older than all the other students. Later I realized why God had us start out with only one attendee.

I did the magic show, we ate, and I did the Bible story. Then I felt like God said, "Go over a tract with her." I obeyed and when we got to the end, I asked Sarah, "Have you ever prayed a prayer inviting Jesus into your life?"

"No I haven't," the teen responded.

"Would you like to now?" I quizzed.

"Yes!" led us to pray a prayer of repentance and acceptance of Jesus as her Lord and Savior.

Sarah was so excited that she instantly told her mom and younger sister when they picked her up. Her mom called to thank me. "It was Jesus who drew her and told me to go over the tract with Sarah. He also had her be the only one who came so she wouldn't be distracted by the other students," I responded. Sarah was baptized a few days later.

67

If there had been a lot of little kids around, I don't believe that Sarah would have received Christ. All the other Activity Days have been larger. After a year and a half, Sarah went back to live with her father. She was caught up in her math and began to enjoy the subject. Her reading was already ahead of level because she loved to read so much. Sarah was also caught up in the rest of her subjects when she left and had developed better study skills. She got to go up to her grade level and to take Jesus back home with her.

Many other miracles have happened through the ministry, but the biggest miracles have happened in my heart. I have learned to trust even when the storms have me underwater gasping for breath.

Abraham didn't wait on God's timing and had Ishmael before the promised son, Isaac. God cornered me in, with the mental illness, and I had no choice but to wait. I became a prisoner in my own room. As I recovered, I would always fulfill commitments or have the strength to cancel those that were not required. Then, I would become a pile of emotional mush, as the stress slammed down on me.

When God's clock said "Wait," wait I did because I had no choice. I had freely given my will to Him years before the mental break. I saw Him working when I tried to rush. He'd say "Wait," and then make it happen by confining me to my bed. Waiting in God is not burdensome. I'm not lazy. He had plenty for me to do while waiting and just abiding in Him. I spent time reading His word, praying for others and for guidance, writing, planning, witnessing to clients at doctors' offices, and whatever else He'd have me do.

Continually Wounded

The effects of the church discipline have never totally ended. Sometimes everyone seemingly acts normal. At other times my world is a nightmare of emotional and mental cruelty, hurled by everyone around me. Some of my family snubs me at a family gathering one minute, and then the next minute asks if I'm O.K., knowing that I'm not and knowing why. As everyone is leaving, they hug me and tell me they love me, but love isn't cruel. When all is quiet my mind screams for order out of chaos. My emotions plead, "What have I done to cause everyone to react to me as if programmed by an alien monster?"

Then the tears stream down my face and God wraps His loving arms around me and I am at peace in Him. Jesus and Jesus alone loves me unconditionally.

The pill I'd taken earlier takes effect and the flashbacks, weird sensation in my brain, and paranoia leave. But questions remain. "Will I ever be confident of any human love if all can be ripped away within one minute's time?" Love says I'm sorry when it wrongs another. I never hear I'm sorry. I say it often, but others never do. My mind and emotions need answers. What have I done to evoke such horror? I can forgive instantly now but can never feel like it is finally over. Hundreds of times I had believed that it was over and let fall tears of relief. Now, I forgive and love knowing that it will never be over. I will never hear, "I'm sorry," or never have answers to "Why?'

Love will never be restored to me. Love talks about everything, the pain and the joy, the laughter and the tears, but I am supposed to accept insanity as sanity, the cruel as kindness, hate as love, and discipline as normal.

Medicine and God are my only recourse. Living in Hell one day or minute, then living in acceptance the next, seems to be my lot in life. So I write to whoever will read, and I pray and I am heard. I pray and am heard and loved by the King of all kings. Then I can love and accept the beings that I don't understand. The pain is gone until next time.

Now at peace, I meditate on Your love, my Lord. You loved me enough to live as a human and to die in my place for all my sins. Not only my sins, but for those done against me. I don't have to be as one with them, but only with thee.

Tomorrow I will act normally and hopefully be treated normally. But, it doesn't matter because I have learned that if God is all you have then God is more than enough. Love Himself came down from Heaven for me. Love Himself came down from Heaven for them. So in you Lord Jesus, I can be one in them because you love them through me. It doesn't matter how I am treated, it only matters how I respond. I choose to love because you first loved me. I rest in you and in your love.

Meditate on Jesus

"Now also when I am old and gray headed, O God, forsake me not; until I have shewed thy strength unto this generation, and thy power to every one that is to come." (Psalm 71:18)

"For I am persuaded, that neither death, nor life, nor angels, nor principalities, nor powers, nor things present, nor things to come, Nor height, nor depth, nor any other creature, shall be able to separate us from the love of God, which is in Christ Jesus our Lord." (Romans 8:38-39)

"For I reckon that the sufferings of this present time are not worthy to be compared with the glory which shall be revealed in us." (Romans 8:18)

"Can a woman forget her suckling child, that she should not have compassion on the son of her womb? Yea, they may forget, yet will I not forget thee. Behold I have graven thee upon the palms of my hands... (Isaiah 49:15-16)

I waited patiently for the Lord; and he inclined unto me, and heard my cry. He brought me up also out of an horrible pit, out of the miry clay, and set my foot upon a rock, and established my goings." (Psalm 40:1-2)

"And she shall bring forth a son, and thou shalt call his name JESUS: for he shall save his people from their sins. (Matthew 1:21)

"Blessed be God, even the Father of our Lord Jesus Christ, The Father of mercies, and the God of all comfort; Who comforteth us in all our tribulation, that we may be able to comfort them which are in any trouble, by the comfort wherewith we ourselves are comforted of God. For as the sufferings of Christ abound in us, so our consolation also aboundeth by Christ. And whether we be afflicted, it is for your consolation and salvation, which is effectual in the enduring of the same sufferings which we also suffer: or whether we be comforted, it is for your consolation and salvation. And our hope of you is steadfast, knowing, that as ye are partakers of the sufferings, so shall ye be also of the consolation." (II Corinthians 1:3-7)

"Be careful for nothing; but in every thing by prayer and supplication with thanksgiving let your request be made known unto God. And the peace of God, which passeth all understanding, shall keep your hearts and minds through Christ Jesus." (Philippians 4:6-7)

"For we have not an high priest which cannot be touched with the feelings of our infirmities; but was in all points tempted like as we are, yet without sin. Let us therefore come boldly unto the throne of grace, that we may obtain mercy, and find grace to help in time of need." (Hebrews 4:15-16)

"To every thing there is a season, and a time to every purpose under the heaven: A time to be born, and a time to die; a time to plant, and a time to pluck up that which is planted; A time to kill, and a time to heal; a time to break down, and a time to build up; A time to weep, and a time to laugh; a time to mourn, and a time to dance; A time to cast away stones, and a time to gather stones together; a time to embrace, and a time to refrain from embracing; A time to get, and a time to lose; a time to keep, and a time to cast away; A time to rend, and a time to sew; a time to keep silent, and a time to speak; A time to love, and a time to hate; a time of war, and a time of peace." (Ecclesiastes 3:1-8)

"Thou tellest my wanderings: put thou my tears into thy bottle: are they not in thy book? When I cry unto thee, then shall mine enemies turn back: this I know; for God is for me. In God will I praise his word: in the Lord will I praise his word. In God have I put my trust; I will not be afraid what man can do unto me." (Psalm 56:8-11)

"For I know the thoughts that I think toward you, saith the Lord, thoughts of peace, and not of evil, to give you an expected end." (Jeremiah 29:11)

By whom also we have access by faith into this grace wherein we stand, and rejoice in hope of the glory of God. And not only so, but we glory in tribulation also: knowing that tribulation worketh patience; and patience, experience; and experience, hope; And hope maketh not ashamed; because the love of God is shed abroad in our hearts by the Holy Ghost which is given unto us." (Romans 5:2-5)

"And I, if I be lifted up from the earth, will draw all men unto me." (John 12:32)

"Hear, O Israel: The Lord our God is one Lord: And thou shalt love the Lord thy God with all thine heart, and with all thy soul, and with all thy might. And these words, which I command thee this day, shall be in thine heart:" (Deuteronomy 6:4-6)

"Ye have heard that it hath been said, Thou shall love thy neighbor, and hate thine enemy. But I say unto you, Love your enemies, bless them that curse you, do good to them that hate you, and pray for them which despitefully use you, and persecute you; That ye may be the children of your Father which is in heaven:..." (Matthew 5:43-45)

"And Jesus answered him, The first of all commandments is, Hear O Israel; the Lord our God is one Lord; And thou shalt love the Lord thy God with all thy Heart, and with all thy soul, and with all thy mind, and with all thy strength: this is the first commandment. And the second is like, namely this, Thou shalt love thy neighbor as thyself. There is none other commandment greater than these." (Mark 12: 29-31)

"As the Father hath loved me, so have I loved you: continue ye in my love." (John 15:9)

"If ye abide in me, and my words abide in you, ye shall ask what ye will, and it shall be done unto you. Herein is my Father glorified, that ye bear much fruit; so shall ye be my disciples. As the Father hath loved me, so have I loved you: continue ye in my love." (John 15:7-9)

"I am crucified with Christ: nevertheless I live; yet not I, but Christ liveth in me: and the life which I now live in the flesh I live by the faith of the Son of God, who loved me, and gave himself for me." (Galatians 2:20)

"For we are his workmanship, created in Christ Jesus unto good works, which God hath before ordained that we should walk in them." (Ephesians 2:10)

"Beloved, let us love one another: for love is of God; and every one that loveth is born of God, and knoweth God." (I John 4:7)

Where is My Focus

No one ever got over a problem by focusing on the problem. Then where should our focus be? On Jesus! He said, "If I be lifted up I will draw all men unto me." (John 12:32.) Looking at the problem leads to heartache, pain, and despair. Lifting Jesus up, lifts us up to be with Him. Thus, we are lifted out of the pit of sin, grief, depression, pride, greed, loneliness, or whatever drags us down.

You can only be healed from sin and the results of living in a sinful world by the Great Physician. Christ uses people to accomplish His purposes, too. But, man is limited in what he can do. Even with the help of doctors, teachers, farmers, and others that help meet our needs, it is only through Jesus that they are able to provide the medication, education, and food that we need. He even chooses to work through non-believers, at times, to accomplish His purpose and to receive the glory for all that mankind has done or will ever do.

You've seen the bumper sticker that says, "Jesus is the answer." There is also a bumper sticker that says, "If Jesus is the answer, what is the question?" It doesn't matter what the problem or what the question, Jesus is still the answer. Someone might try to word things in such a way to try to trap us by asking something like: "If I get cut what comes out?" Of course the answer is "blood." But who made the blood? Jesus! Why do I not bleed to death from every cut? Jesus made blood to clot. Why do I get cuts and scrapes? Because we live in a fallen world where the results of sin are clearly seen. But, Jesus died to take away my sins and to heal my wounds. So, if I get cut what comes out is Jesus if we are a child of God; and cursing and yelling if we are not believers.

Another trick question might be: Who cheated on their English test today? The answer could be Tom or Jane, but the answer is also Jesus because He died to take away the sins of the world. So the answer to any question pertaining to a sin is Jesus. When I accept His free gift, I no longer have any sin but His righteousness. No, Christ never sinned. Yes, He took on Himself all the sins of everyone that has ever lived. When I lie or cheat on a test, He paid for that. It is our Lord who became guilty, not those who have accepted that free gift.

Focusing on my Lord makes the problem small enough to pick up and put in my pocket. It is no longer I who carries the weight of the problem but my Master.

If I ask a one year old child to lift a hundred pound bag of feed, it will be impossible. Let's suppose the child's father is a world-class body builder. The 100 pound weight will be no challenge for him. Likewise, our Heavenly Father holds not only the whole world in His Hands but all the infinite number of galaxies as well. So would my problem be too heavy for Him? No way! No matter how big the problem, my God is bigger still.

When my mental illness gets me down, the devil tries to put the focus on me and on the problem. But, I always pull back, spend quality time with God, and am healed by His holy presence. My Jesus was lifted up on the cross so He could be lifted up to Heaven. Now in good times and in bad times, I run to Him. He lifts me high above this world's trials and I lean upon His chest, listening to the soft voice coming from His heart that says, "I love you."

Honesty

My aunt went to the nursing home for a while. Visiting her on the third day after her arrival was the best gift the two of us could have ever had.

We'd been having good conversations lately and this day was no different, except she was feeling that God was going to take her home soon. As I was leaving, I bent down to her wheelchair and hugged her. She said, "Rebecca, I love you. I always have." Her heart broke, and her eyes poured tears.

"I love you too and I always have. We used to be so close. I don't understand what I did to make everyone mad at me," I responded in a broken tone.

She hugged me tighter and cried harder. "It wasn't you, it wasn't any one person, it just happened. Not everyone was mad, just some were. Let's just cry together." Her words broke me, and I cried with her as we held each other as if we were hugging for all those lost years.

I got us some tissue and proclaimed, "God is going to restore all the years the locust have eaten away."

"I believe that," she replied.

"It's a promise," I assured her.

"Yes, it's a promise," ended her tears. "You never did anything, it just happened, it wasn't you. I'll never let it happen to us again," she assured me. When I left, we left each other as close as if all those distant years had never happened.

"You shall know the truth and the truth shall make you free." (John 8:32) The truth is that most people did act cruel toward me, but no one deliberately caused it. Satan used one little lie about me to snowball into many lies and much anger. Then my mind broke and my disturbing and sometimes frightening behavior pushed people farther away. Misunderstanding and lack of communication leads to fear and fear divides. "Perfect love casts out fear." (I John 4:18)

"The devil came to kill, to steal, and to destroy. (John 10:10) But let's not give him all the credit. Satan can do nothing unless it is sifted through God's hands of love. Like I wrote earlier, I'd prayed Philippians 3:10 as a prayer. It says, "That I may know him and the power of his resurrection and the fellowship of his sufferings." God heard that prayer and it was His love and grace that allowed the devil to try me. The Lord knew that when I was tested my faith would be stronger, and in the end, I would love Him deeper and trust Him with all my being.

Ever since I gave my life to Jesus, I have believed that God and relationships were all that was important. Now I know that a relationship with Jesus is all that is important. He can love others through me even when those people do not love me back. I never gave up, though. I believed in God's goodness and love. Now, I am grateful for all the broken years. Grateful for all the shattered lives He could touch through me, because I too, was in a million little pieces. Grateful for His comfort, which I now use to comfort others. (II Corinthians 1:3-7)

If I had not suffered to the extent that I could do nothing but curl up in Jesus' arms, then I could not comfort other crushed people, people with mental illness, grieving people, homeless people, dying people.

The hundreds that He has touched through me in the past 30 plus years make it all worthwhile. I would not go back and undo the past, even if it were possible. Broken relationships can be instantly healed by Christ. God promised me the return of my family at the beginning of my mental and emotional break, and that promise He is fulfilling.

Would I do it all over again? I don't think that I could stand it all again, but I would never take a moment of the excruciating pain away. It has all been to push me closer to the heart of God, to lead many to Him, and to prepare me for His other promises. The promises that God whispered in my ear when I lay crying against His chest. The promises that He would use me for His glory, in His way, His timing, and with His Hands through me.

This vessel (body) is now empty, ready to be filled, and expecting to see great things. As Zechariah 4:6 says, "not by might, nor by power, but by my Spirit, saith the Lord of hosts." Your way Lord. Your time. Through me. I yield you my all.

Thank you God for beauty from ashes. Thank you Jesus for shedding your precious blood for me. Thank you for taking all my sins, pain, and every awful part of me upon yourself. Thank you for giving me your righteousness. Thank you for your love and grace. Grace so undeserved, love so deep that Hell itself cannot separate me from it. I love you because you first loved me. You loved me even while I was a great sinner. Your love is too wonderful to comprehend. Thank you for trials and for deliverance.

Not Alone

I finally got to the point that I didn't need human love because 80% - 90% of my time was spent with God in His arms and with Him in the harvest field. He has given me close friends as He ministers through me. Friends that I can understand where they are coming from and friends who can understand where I have been, because they too, have been there.

All my closest friends have a mental illness. They accept me and love me as I am, as God has made me, with tears and with joy. They love me unconditionally because God loves them through me. I am not bothered by their addictions, paranoia, or hallucinations, because God in His mercy took what the devil did in my life and uses it for His glory and their good. I can love them with the same love that Jesus loved me with. We don't judge each other because all of us are in the same leaky boat. But praise God, Jesus keeps plugging up the leaks with His precious blood.

Before my mental break, God taught me to have compassion for those with mental illness. My Grandmother also had schizophrenia and we were never allowed to be around her when we were growing up, even though she lived in our house part of the time. When in high school, after getting my driver's license, I took my grandmother shopping often. We became very close friends. It bothered her that she was a burden on my father and her daughter. Although they loved her, the responsibility of her often needing much care was too much, along with kids and their jobs. My grandmother and I often teased about her marrying a rich man who had a rich grandson who I would marry. Then the two of us would travel and shop all over the world!

I did have a red-headed soldier, Butch, that I planned to marry when I finished college. We dreamed of living in a big white two-story house with a whole yard full of children, a dog, and a station wagon. I also planned to take my grandmother to live with us. In that way, we would continue to be close and she would feel truly wanted. But, in my freshman year of college, I lost my grandmother to a brain hemorrhage and Butch to the Vietnam War.

Since getting well to the point that I can take care of myself and stable enough to minister to others, I have become a conservator for Vivian, who has a mental illness, had been homeless, was in danger of losing her housing again, and couldn't take care of herself. That led to doing two Bible studies for people who have been homeless and have special needs, including mental illness.

I also get to know many people who have a mental illness while waiting for my psychiatric appointments. I told one doctor who asked, "What have you been doing to keep busy?"

"Oh, I've just been counseling your patients," was my reply.

"Good," he responded.

I also met many of my friends at Stepping Stones, a rehabilitation center for people with a mental illness. I went there for many years to take computer classes and many more years to volunteer to tutor in computer and GED classes.

So called "normal" people really miss out on a lot that God has to offer by picking and choosing their own friends. God can grow us up a lot through the love and sorrow that is in the hearts of people many consider "low life". By judging others we are judging ourselves and missing out on all that everyone has to offer us. The neediest people are usually the most loving also. The compassion in their hearts comes from suffering, and the sorrow comes from losing most of their family and friends. With the help of medication and God, they are "normal" except more loving and forgiving than their "normal" family members.

Besides Job and other Bible people being my friends, so are the homeless, the outcast, and the hurting of this world. These are the same friends that Jesus had. He loves us all, but Christ and others receive the most love back from those who have suffered, really suffered – beyond comprehension.

I don't cry now, have flashbacks, or have a startled sensation in my brain anymore, because Jesus is my whole life. Each day He ministers love to me and most days, He allows me to minister that same love to others. Sometimes that love is returned and sometimes that love is withheld. I am usually at peace now no matter what. Paranoia and thinking others are being controlled to emotionally wound me no longer control my mind, will, and emotions. I no longer have to grieve over the pain, and there is nothing to forgive because peace resides in me. I read a book, Tortured for Christ, by Richard Wurmbrand with The Voice of the Martyrs Ministry which was very helpful. He and other Christians were imprisoned for their faith in communist countries. They never lost their love or compassion for their torturers no matter how sadistic the torment. Their only thoughts were to witness and to pray for their captors. He realized the pain in the unbelievers was greater than his own because he had Jesus. He loved the prison guards with Christ's love and nothing the tormentors could do could take away that love. What a testimony!

One friend said that I had "matured" when I explained my feelings now. However it is not maturing but lying in the arms of Jesus and letting Him carry me – it is not my love or Pastor Wurmbrand's love but the love of God flowing through us. This world no longer has any hold on me. I don't need money, things, people, family, health, kindness, nothing but Jesus. I am grateful for all He gives me, including air to breathe, a good night's sleep, useful things to do, and peace even during the storms. If my boat goes under, He goes under with me. If I live, it is for Him. If I die, He will be there waiting for me.

I will never feel lonely again because Jesus' presence is ever-present and constant. I am at peace, content, and even full of joy in my world, even when the nightmare of paranoia is going on. Neither Satan nor any man has power over me any longer. The person inside, the person who is in Jesus, and Christ in me, is now free from the effects of this world's evil. I may have another mental break, but I do not fear what may come because I know who holds my future – my best friend, Jesus!

Bigger and Better

We are now in the process of expanding the ministry. I stay active most of the time. With no T.V., work is a form of relaxation and enjoyment. I minister one on one, do workshops and speaking engagements for church groups, colleges, NAMI, and whoever wants to hear what God has given me to say. Other volunteers and I tutor several children. I write, plan and carry out conferences, hold Activity Days, and everything else I believe that God would have me do.

My Lord is opening many doors. I am always running into someone that I hadn't seen for years. They wind up being a big connection to lots of churches, even churches in different states. He is also working miracles in the fundraising department. Two ladies began donating aluminum cans to sell without even being asked. Three people donated things to sell at flea markets, while cleaning out their houses. Donations also come in from unexpected places. I gave this book to a friend before it was completed because she has a sister with a mental illness. She read it then sent it to her mother who donated $50 because she felt that it was so helpful in understanding her daughter's medical condition.

I don't try to raise money anymore, but pray and wait on God. When I was trying to raise funds, we kept getting deeper in the hole. God uses funds or lack of them to direct us in what He wants us to do or what we are to back off from doing. His will is perfect, and a closed door somewhere means an open door somewhere else. When I try to do things in the flesh, then I fall right on my face. When I pray, trust, and wait on God to do through me or through someone else, then He gets all the glory and I stand amazed at all He does.

My tears are now only Godly tears for the lost and compassion for others who hurt. The few tears are but for a moment as I yield myself to be useful in God's harvest field. I still take my medications, see my psychiatrist and other doctors, get enough rest, exercise, and spend much time in God's word, so I can stay mentally and physically whole. I am healed through God's gift of wisdom to those who have discovered the right medications, His presence to bring peace, contentment, patience and love.

There truly is a light at the end of mental illness, and that light opens up a whole world of possibilities. Jesus is that light and nothing can extinguish it. For months I have gone steadily forward with no retreats. As long as I hold on to God's hand and allow Him to do the work through me, life will be beautiful every day, even when it is storming. Lasting peace is possible no matter what the circumstances and no matter how severe your mental, emotional, and physical break may be. God is in control. Trust Him. Put yourself in His Hands and in His will and be overwhelmed every day by all He does.

God Bless You and keep you close to His heart.

Made in the USA
Lexington, KY
01 December 2019